Real-life maths

This book belongs to
....

Colour the star when you complete a page.
See how far you've come!

Author: Sarah-Anne Fernandes

How to use this book

- This book takes a thematic approach to real-world maths to engage your child with maths that they can recognise in their everyday life.
- Find a quiet, comfortable place to work, away from distractions.
- Make sure your child has some paper to write their ideas and workings on.
- Help with reading the instructions where necessary and ensure that your child understands what to do.
- Within each theme there are lots of problem-solving and reasoning activities for your child to complete. Your child will have to select and apply the appropriate number, measurement, geometry and/or statistics skills to solve each problem.
- Always end each activity before your child gets tired so that they will be eager to return next time.
- Help and encourage your child to check their own answers as they complete each activity.
- Let your child return to their favourite pages once they have been completed. Talk about the activities they enjoyed and what they have learnt.
- Reward your child with plenty of praise and encouragement.

Special features of this book:

- **Progress chart:** when your child has completed a page, ask them to colour in the relevant star on the first page of the book. This will enable you to keep track of progress through the activities and help to motivate your child.

- **Learning tip:** situated in a yellow box at the bottom of the page, this offers further guidance, suggests further activities and encourages discussion about what your child has learnt.

Published by Collins
An imprint of HarperCollins*Publishers* Ltd
The News Building
1 London Bridge Street
London SE1 9GF

HarperCollins*Publishers*
Macken House, 39/40 Mayor Street Upper,
Dublin 1, D01 C9W8, Ireland

© HarperCollins*Publishers* Ltd 2026

10 9 8 7 6 5 4 3 2 1

ISBN 978-0-00-877529-2

The author asserts the moral right to be identified as the author of this work.

All rights reserved. No part of this publication may be reproduced, stored in a retrieval system, or transmitted, in any form or by any means, electronic, mechanical, photocopying, recording or otherwise, without the prior permission of Collins.

Without limiting the exclusive rights of any author, contributor or the publisher of this publication, any unauthorised use of this publication to train generative artificial intelligence (AI) technologies is expressly prohibited. HarperCollins also exercise their rights under Article 4(3) of the Digital Single Market Directive 2019/790 and expressly reserve this publication from the text and data mining exception.

British Library Cataloguing in Publication Data

A Catalogue record for this publication is available from the British Library.

Author: Sarah-Anne Fernandes
Publisher: Fiona McGlade
Editor: Katie Galloway
Cover design: Sarah Duxbury and Amparo Barrera
Interior concept design: Ian Wrigley
Page layouts: QBS Learning and Sarah Duxbury
Production: Bethany Brohm
All images ©Shutterstock.com and ©HarperCollins*Publishers*
Printed in the UK

Contents

At the fruit and vegetable stall	4
Going to school	8
Weather and temperature	12
Visiting the aquarium	16
Keeping healthy	18
Saving up	20
In the kitchen	22
In the garden	26
Playing games	30
Answers	32

At the fruit and vegetable stall

You are at the market buying fruit and vegetables. You need to understand weights and fractions and be able to use money to pay.

1 Circle the coins you need to buy each piece of fruit.

- Apple — 24p
- Banana — 72p
- Orange — 31p
- Pear — 62p

2 Draw the coins you need to buy this box of vegetables.

£3 and 75p

Your child needs to be able to recognise coins and identify the value of each coin. It may be helpful to take a coin and show its value using 1p coins. For example, a 5p coin is equal to five 1p coins.

3 Some fruits and vegetables are being weighed.
What mass is shown on each scale?

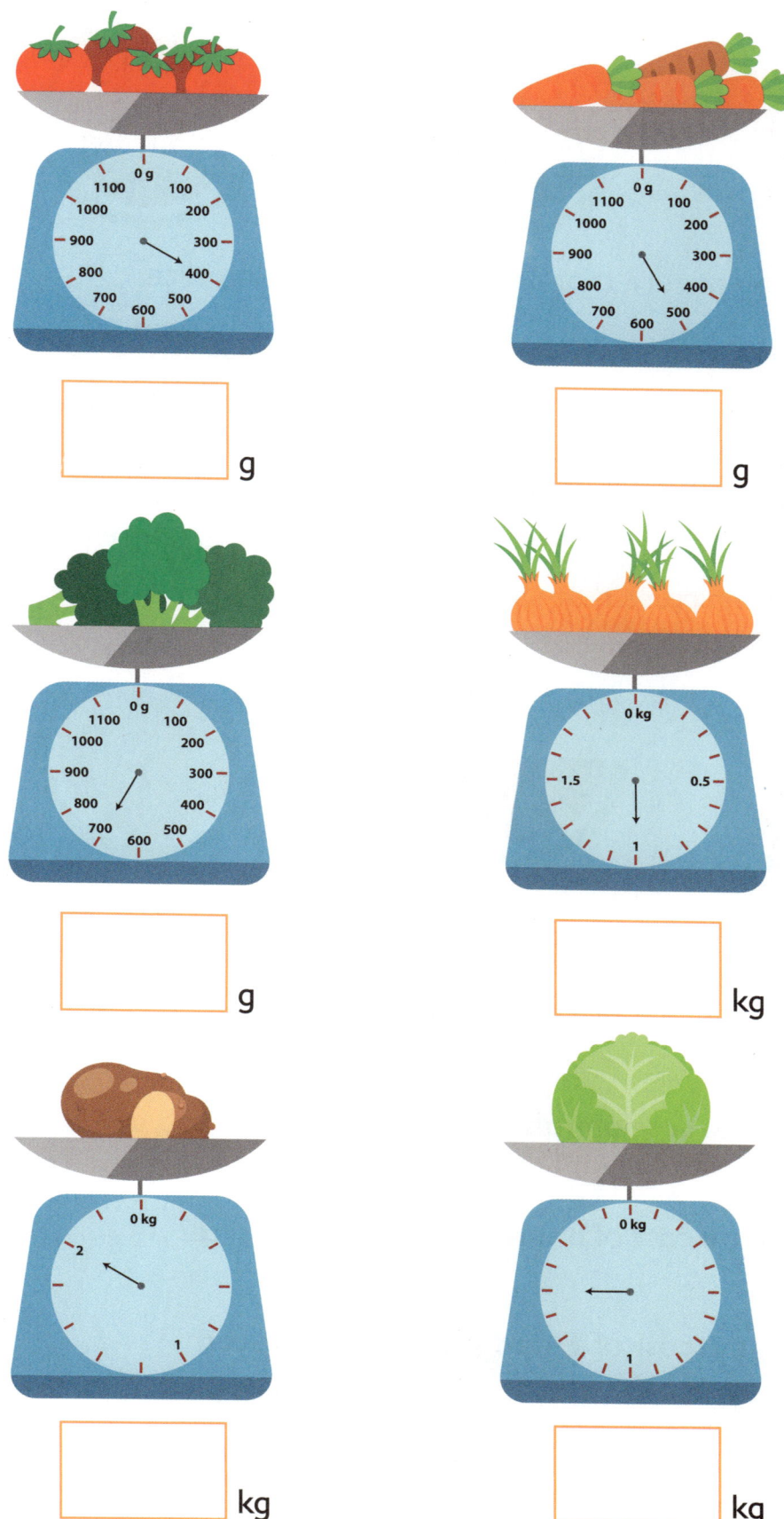

4 Melon slices are sold as whole, half and a quarter.
   Circle the picture that shows a **whole** melon slice.

Circle the picture that shows **half** of a melon slice.

Circle the picture that shows a **quarter** of a melon slice.

5 The cost of **2 whole** melon slices is £4.

What is the cost of **1 whole** melon slice? £ ☐

What is the cost of **half** a melon slice? £ ☐

What is the cost of a **quarter** of a melon slice? ☐ p

What is the cost of **1 and a half** melon slices? £ ☐

> Your child needs to be able to recognise a whole, half and a quarter. It is important to explain that two halves are equal and that a quarter is not just one of four parts, but that each part must be equal. So, a half is one of two *equal* parts; a quarter is one of four *equal* parts.

6 The prices are shown for these pieces of fruit.

apple 20p, banana 40p, orange 30p, pear 35p, plum 10p

Find the **total cost** of each set of fruit.

apple + orange: ☐ P

pear + plum: ☐ P

banana + apple + orange: ☐ P

You pay for each set of fruit with £1.
How much **change** do you get?

☐ P   ☐ P   ☐ P

Draw **three different** sets of fruit that total £1 each.

☐   ☐   ☐

Help your child to understand that finding the total cost involves addition, and working out change involves subtraction. Try using role play to buy items and work out change from a £1 coin.

Going to school

You are getting ready to go to school. You need to be organised to do things in the correct order, follow and give directions and tell the time so you are not late.

1 Use each of these words to complete the sentences to describe how you get ready for school.

Next   Finally   Thirdly   Secondly   After that   First

1 _____, I get out of bed.	2 _____, I get dressed.
3 _____, I eat my breakfast.	4 _____, I brush my teeth.
5 _____, I pack my school bag.	6 _____, I set off to school.

2 Draw hands on the clocks to show the times given below.

Mia gets out of bed at 7 o'clock.

She gets dressed at 10 minutes past 7.

Mia eats her breakfast at half past 7.

She brushes her teeth at quarter to 8.

Mia packs her school bag at 5 minutes past 8.

She leaves home at quarter past 8.

Your child needs to be able to read the time to the nearest 5 minutes on an analogue clock. Practise reading the time on a clock with them, for example, 3 o'clock, quarter past 3, half past 3, quarter to 4, then 5 past, 10 past, 20 past, 25 past but also 25 minutes to, 10 minutes to, etc.

3) Sam chooses these items for his lunch box.
Write the 3-D shape name for each item.

_____   _____   _____

4) The table shows the days that Mia wears uniform to school.
The other days she wears her PE kit.

Monday	Uniform
Wednesday	Uniform
Thursday	Uniform

What days of the week does Mia wear her PE kit?

_____ and _____

5) These are Mia's uniform items.

A B C D

List all the possible ways Mia can wear her uniform.

_____ with _____

_____ with _____

_____ with _____

_____ with _____

6 Sam gets the number seventeen bus to school.

Circle the bus he needs to take.

Sam gets on the bus at half past 8 in the morning.
He gets off at 10 minutes to 9 in the morning.

How long was the bus journey? ☐ minutes

Sam gets to school at 09:00. Assembly is at 09:15

How long does he have to wait until assembly? ☐ minutes

7 Mia walks from home to the bus stop.

Fill in the missing directions to help Mia get from home to the bus stop.

Start

Forward 4

_____ 6

_____ 3

Left _____

Your child needs to be able to understand and give directions. Together, practise giving directions using the words, *forwards, backwards, right, left, up, down*. You could also begin to discuss turns – *clockwise, anticlockwise*.

Weather and temperature

The weather and the temperature change throughout the months of the year. Weather can be recorded on charts and pictograms and temperature is shown on a thermometer.

1 Fill in the missing months of the calendar year.

Then draw lines to match the months of the year to each season.

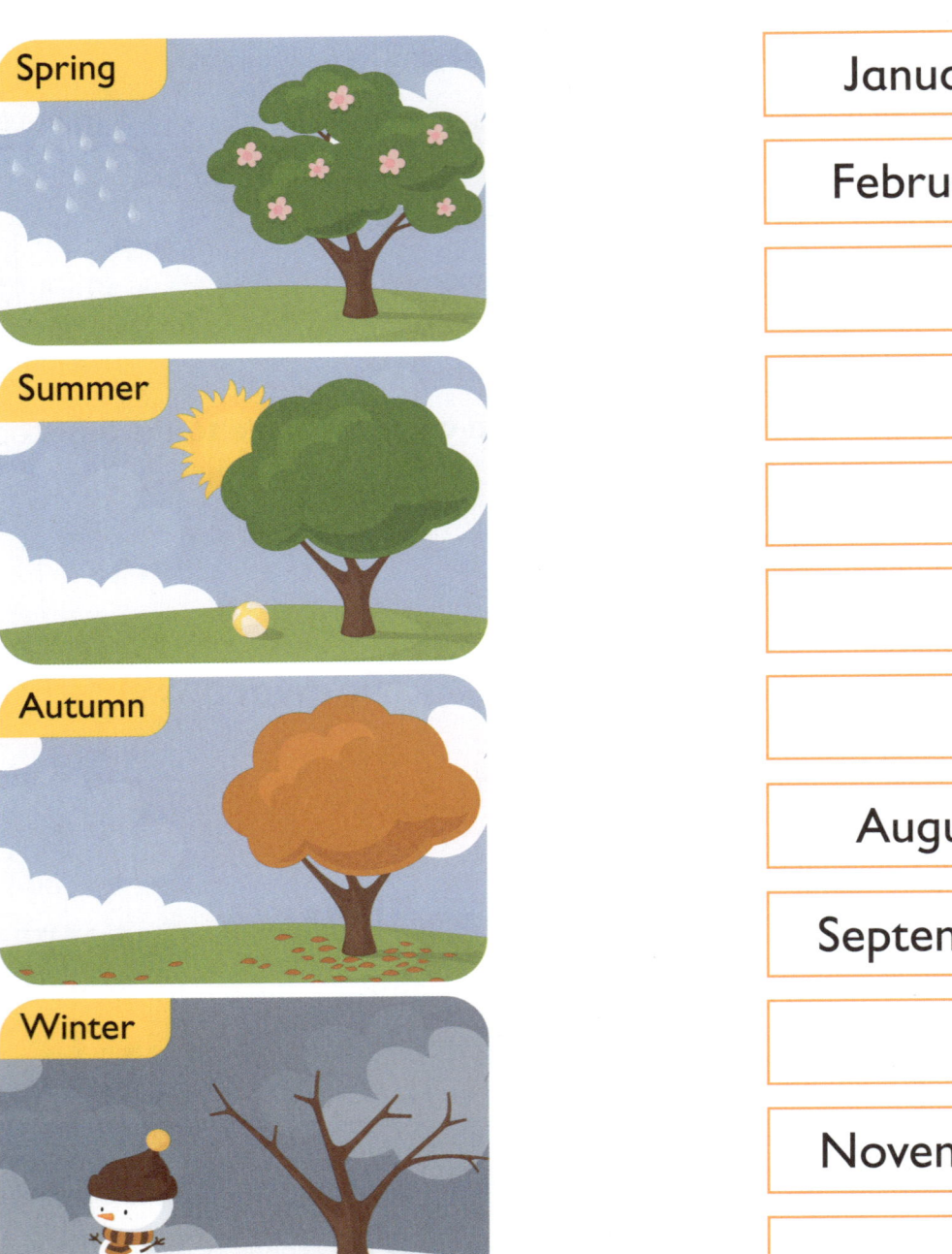

| January |
| February |
| |
| |
| |
| |
| |
| August |
| September |
| |
| November |
| |

2 This calendar page shows the weather each day in the month of April.

Sunday	Monday	Tuesday	Wednesday	Thursday	Friday	Saturday
☀️	☁️	☁️	☁️	🌧️	🌧️	🌧️
🌧️	☁️	☀️	☀️	☀️	☀️	☀️
⚡	⚡	🌧️	🌧️	☀️	☀️	☁️
☀️	🌧️	🌧️	☁️	☀️	☀️	☀️
☀️	☀️					

How many days of the month were sunny? ⬜ days

How many days of the month were cloudy? ⬜ days

How many days of the month had rain? ⬜ days

How many days of the month had thunder and lightning? ⬜ days

How many more days had rain than were cloudy? ⬜ days

How many more days were sunny than had rain? ⬜ days

Tom says, 'In April, half of the month was sunny.'
Explain why Tom is **not** right.

_____

_____

3 The thermometers show the average temperature in different cities in June.

Write the temperature for each city.

Dublin

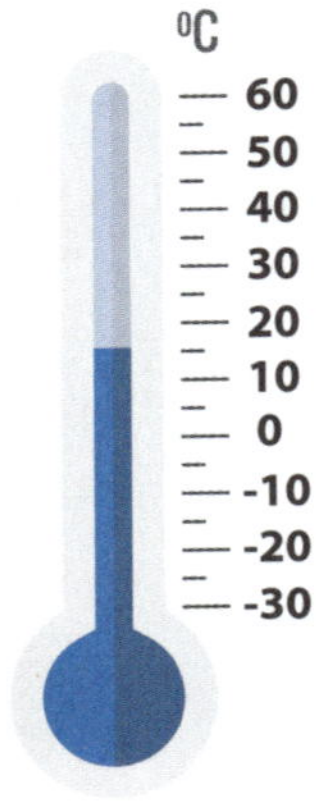

°C

London

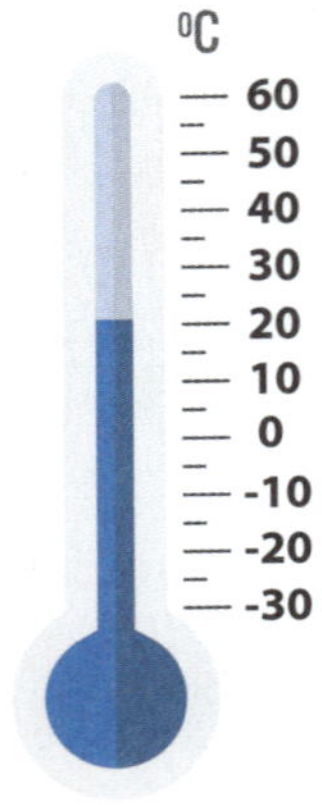

°C

Oslo

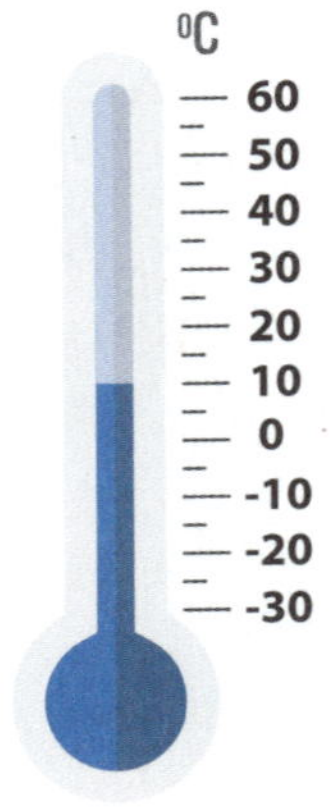

°C

Dubai

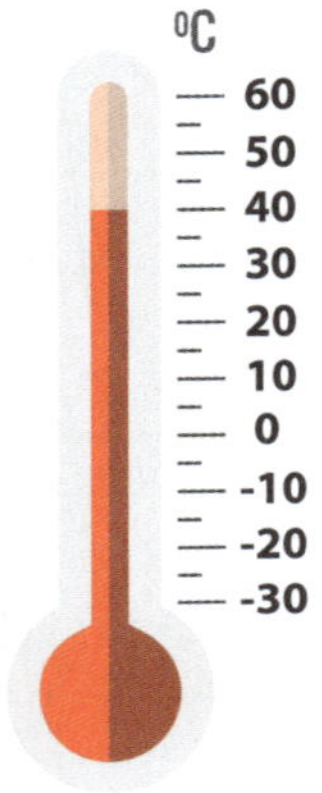

°C

Berlin

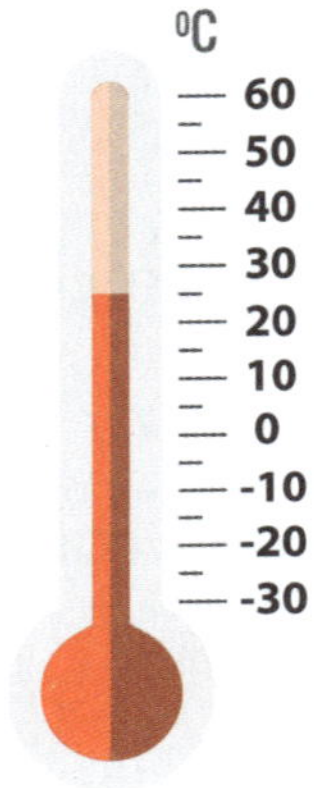

°C

Athens

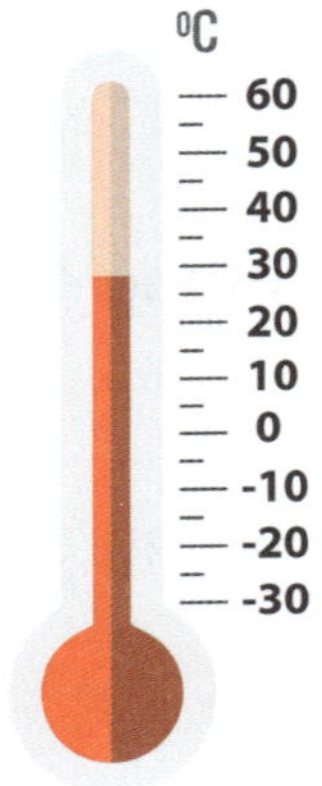

°C

Put the four **warmest** cities in order from hottest to coolest.

What is the difference in temperature between Dubai and London? °C

Your child needs to use language relating to dates, including days of the week, months and years, and how many days are in each calendar month. They also need to be able to read a themometer; this is something you can practise with them at home.

4 This bar chart shows the average rainfall each month in the UK.

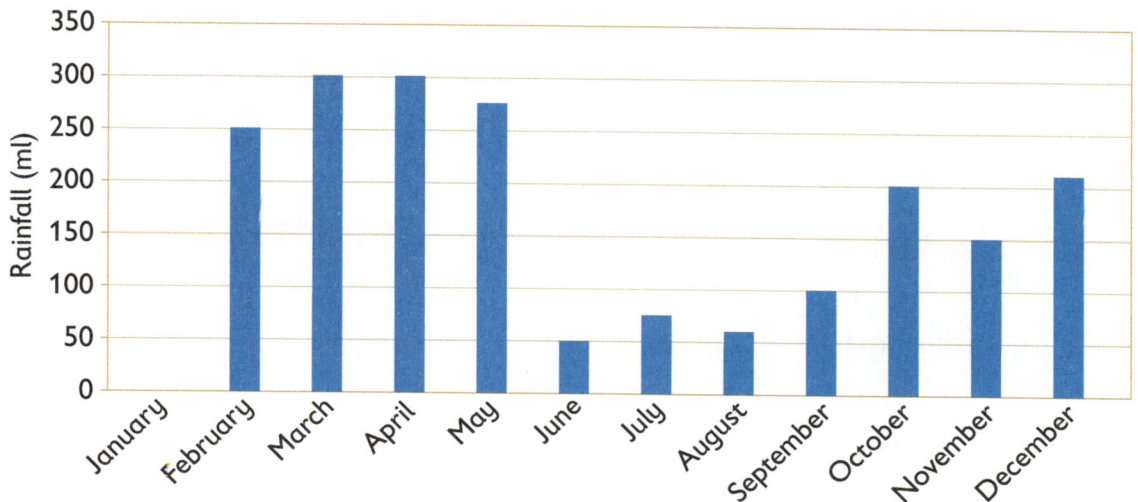

The average rainfall in January is 125 ml.

Complete the bar chart to show rainfall in January.

Which month has the least rainfall? _____

Which two months have the same amount of rainfall?

_____ and _____

What is the total amount of rainfall in September, October and November?

[ ] ml

5 To help combat climate change and look after the environment, we need to recycle as much as we can.

This chart shows the number of cans recycled in a school in one week.

How many cans were recycled?

How many more cans need to be recycled to reach a target of **100 cans**?

Visiting the aquarium

You are visiting the aquarium. There are lots of interesting number facts about the ocean and sea creatures.

1 Write the length of each seahorse.

☐ cm   ☐ cm   ☐ cm

2 Coral reef is a special habitat under the sea. One quarter of sea creatures need this habitat to survive.

Shade one quarter of the bar diagram.

The ocean covers seven tenths (70 percent) of the Earth's surface.

Shade seven tenths of the bar diagram.

Your child needs to be confident using a ruler to measure objects. Demonstrate how to use a ruler to measure by starting at the '0', rather than at the end of the ruler. Measure lengths of string: some whole centimetre lengths (e.g. 7 cm, 12 cm) and some that include half a centimetre (e.g. 6.5 cm).

3) The aquarium puts on sea lion shows every day.
Write the time of each show.

_____   _____   _____

During the shows, each sea lion eats 20 kilograms of fish.
How much fish is eaten by:

2 sea lions? [   ] kg   4 sea lions? [   ] kg

5 sea lions? [   ] kg   10 sea lions? [   ] kg

4) The table shows the lengths of 4 shark species at the aquarium.

Species of shark	Length in feet
Basking shark	35
Great white shark	20
Greenland shark	14
Tiger shark	12

Use the symbols < and > to compare the lengths of the sharks.

Tiger shark [ ] Great white shark

Basking shark [ ] Greenland shark

Greenland shark [ ] Tiger shark

Great white shark [ ] Basking shark

Keeping healthy

You are thinking of ways to keep healthy and strong. You can sort foods into different groups and count in steps when you exercise.

1 You need to eat a balanced diet to keep healthy.
Draw lines to sort each food item into the correct food group.

Bread and pasta

Fruit and vegetables

Meat and beans (protein)

Dairy

Fats and oils

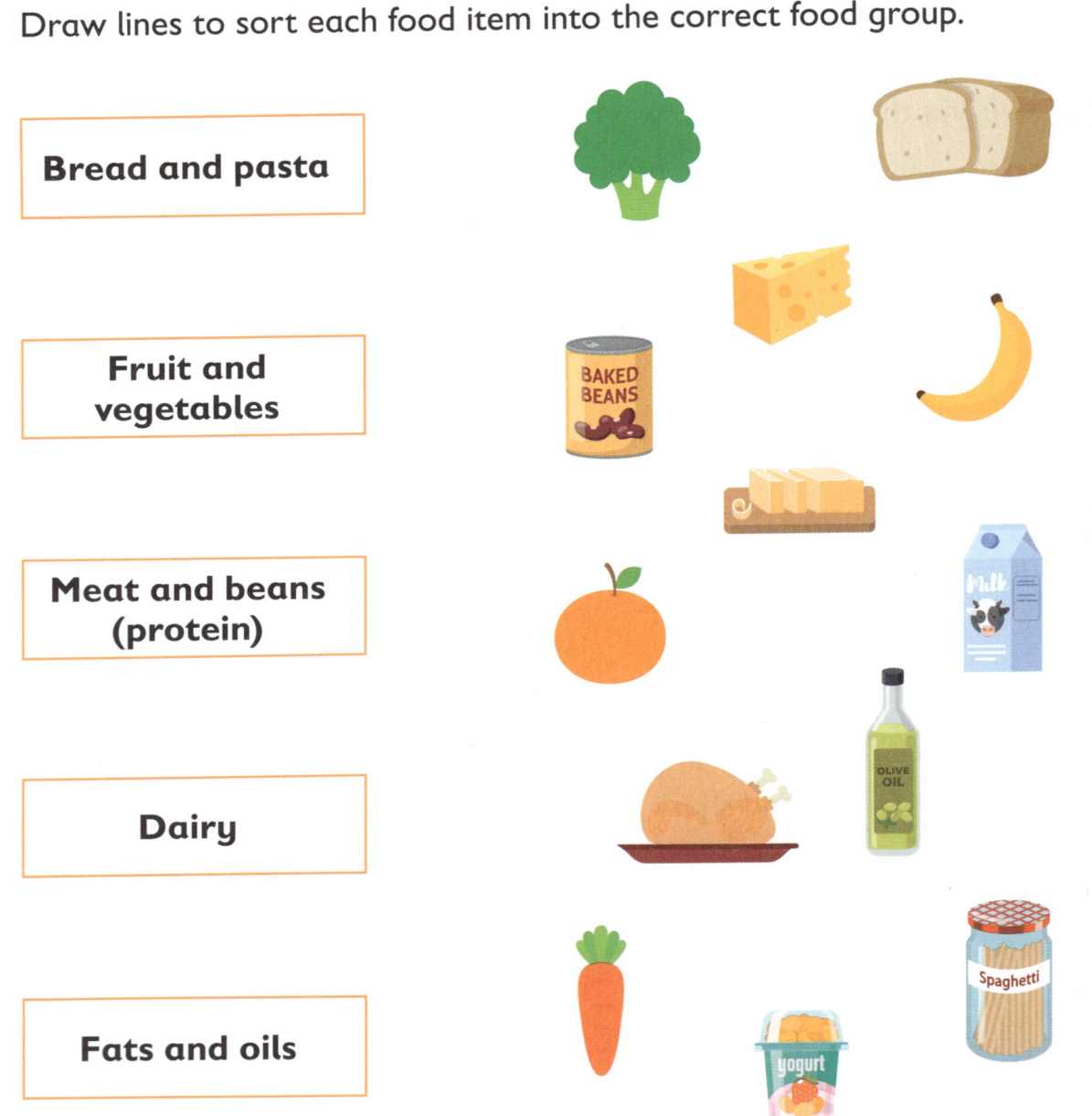

Your child needs to be able to sort and categorise objects, shapes and numbers by their properties. Practise sorting shapes with your child, for example, into 2-D shapes and 3-D shapes. You can also practise sorting numbers into even numbers and odd numbers, or multiples of 2, 5 or 10.

2 Sophie and Billy are skipping to keep fit. They are counting their skips.

Sophie is counting in **2s**. Continue counting her skips.

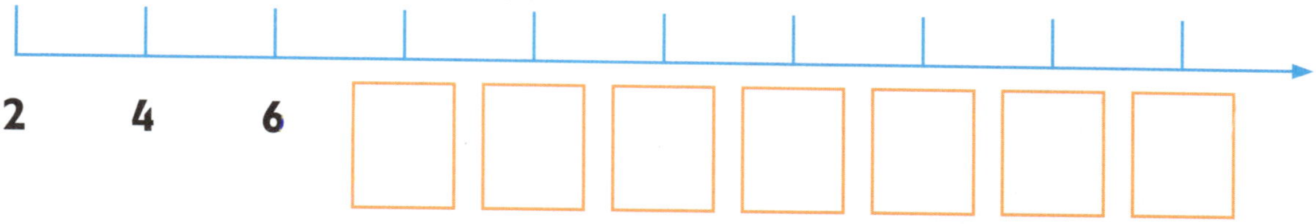

2   4   6

Billy is counting in **10s**. Continue counting his skips.

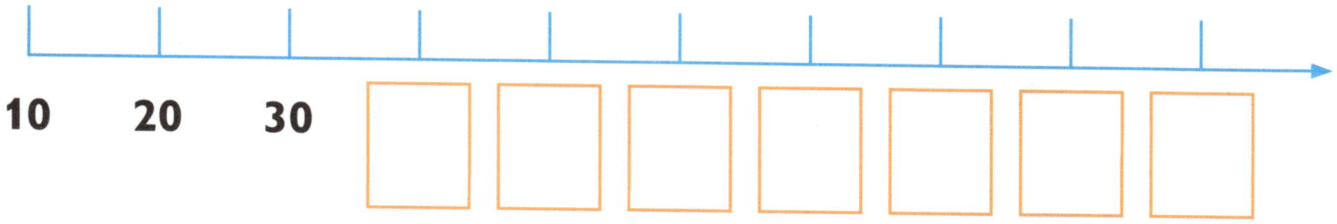

10   20   30

3 The children in Year 1 are choosing healthy snacks. The tally chart shows their choices.

Apple	卌 卌 卌 卌 卌	
Rice cakes	卌 l	
Cucumber	卌 卌 ll	
Milk	卌 卌 卌 lll	
Banana	卌 卌 l	
Carrot	卌 卌	

How many pupils choose milk?

How many pupils choose an apple?

How many more pupils choose cucumber than a banana?

What is the difference between the number of pupils who choose cucumber and the number of pupils who choose rice cakes?

What is the total number of pupils who choose an apple or a carrot?

Saving up

Work out how much money you need in order to buy items in shops and how much money you need to save up to buy things you want.

1 Look at these jars of money.

A 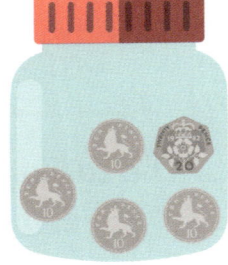   B    C

How much money is saved in each jar?

A:  p   B:  p   C:  p

How much money needs to be added to each jar to total £1?

A:  p   B: _____ p   C:  p

2 You want to buy some items from a shop.

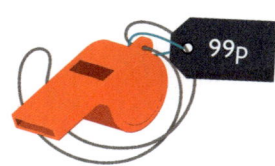 99p    10p    75p

Which money jar above can you use to buy the pencil? _____

How many sweets can you buy using jar A? _____

Can you use one of the money jars to buy the whistle?

Explain your answer.

_____

_____

20

3) You are saving 1p coins.

How many coins do you need to save 50p? ☐ coins

How many coins do you need to save £1? ☐ coins

Isla is saving 10p coins.

How many coins does she need to save 90p? ☐ coins

How many coins does she need to save £1? ☐ coins

4) Rimal is saving up for a new bike. The bike costs £110

Rimal has saved £60. How much more money does she need to save? £ ☐

Rimal is going to save £5 per week. How many weeks will she need to save for to have enough money? ☐ weeks

5) Ari has saved £80. He spends half of this money on books.

He then spends a quarter of the remaining money on a bag.

How much does the bag cost? £ ☐

Your child needs to understand the value of items and how we need to save up our money to buy items. You can practise this skill by giving your child a set amount of money and asking them to look at a catalogue to choose things they can afford to buy and others that they need to save up for.

In the kitchen

Make juices and bake sweet treats in the kitchen! You can work out timings, measure ingredients and understand how to double or halve recipe ingredients to make the correct quantity.

1 You are making a tropical fruit juice. You need:

300 ml apple juice
550 ml pineapple juice
150 ml orange juice

Circle the jug that has the correct amount of apple juice.

Circle the jug that has the correct amount of orange juice.

Circle the jug that has the correct amount of pineapple juice.

What is the total amount of fruit juice that you make?  ml

You pour the fruit juice into 100 ml glasses.
How many glasses can you fill?  glasses

2 Here are the ingredients to make **8** flapjacks:

300 g of oats
80 g of butter
60 g of golden syrup

Orla is making **16** flapjacks. How much of each ingredient will she need?

☐ g of oats   ☐ g of butter   ☐ g of syrup

Henry is making **4** flapjacks. How much of each ingredient will he need?

☐ g of oats   ☐ g of butter   ☐ g of syrup

Savanna is making **12** flapjacks. How much of each ingredient will she need?

☐ g of oats   ☐ g of butter   ☐ g of syrup

3 You put a cake to bake in the oven at 11:20 am.

Show this time on the clock.

The cake needs 1 and a half hours in the oven to bake.

What time will you need to take the cake out of the oven?

_____

Your child needs to be able to read scales to weigh mass, measure liquids and find the height of items. Practise using measuring tools and discuss with your child that it is important to look at the increments going up the scale, e.g. does it go up in 10s or 100s or 50s?

4 Louie bakes trays of biscuits. Fill in the missing numbers in the two equations that match each set.

4 × ☐ = ☐

☐ × 4 = ☐

3 × ☐ = ☐

☐ × 3 = ☐

4 × ☐ = ☐

☐ × 4 = ☐

5 Amelia is baking biscuits.

She takes the biscuits out of the oven at 20 minutes past three o'clock. The biscuits had half an hour in the oven.

What time did Amelia put the biscuits in the oven?

_____

The biscuits need to cool for a quarter of an hour before being iced.

What time can Amelia ice the biscuits?

_____

Your child needs to know the 2, 5 and 10 times tables. Practise creating arrays with your child for each times table fact and discuss how the array can be read in two ways, e.g. 5 × 3 = 15 or 3 × 5 = 15.

6 You have a cake that is cut into 8 equal slices. You and three friends each have 1 slice of cake.

What fraction of the cake is left over?

7 Nell bakes 12 cupcakes.

She puts sprinkles on one third of the cupcakes.

Colour in the bar model to show the fraction of cupcakes that have sprinkles.

8 Joey bakes 25 brownies.

He puts two strawberries on each brownie.

How many strawberries does Joey need? _____ strawberries

Joey puts the brownies in boxes.

Each box holds 5 brownies.

How many boxes does Joey need? _____ boxes

Joey takes 12 brownies to the school bake sale.

He sells each brownie for 50p.

How much money does Joey make? £ _____

Using a bar model is an effective strategy to show your child how to divide a whole into equal parts to find fractions of numbers. Practise making different bar models (e.g. $\frac{1}{2}$, a bar split into two equal parts, or $\frac{1}{4}$, a bar split into four equal parts) and divide the whole between the equal parts to find one part.

In the garden

In the garden, you can enjoy nature, as well as explore patterns and symmetry, look at the position of objects and take measurements.

1 Some small twigs, leaves and stones have been used to make patterns. Draw the next two items in each pattern.

2 You are planting bulbs in plant pots.

You share 35 bulbs equally between 5 pots. How many bulbs do you plant in each pot?

You share 20 bulbs equally between 2 pots. How many bulbs do you plant in each pot?

3 There is a vegetable patch in the garden. Cabbages are planted in 3 rows with 10 cabbages in each row. How many cabbages are planted?

Pumpkins are planted in 5 rows with 4 pumpkins in each row. How many pumpkins are planted?

Your child needs to be able to order numbers considering the place value of each digit in a number. Talk about how many tens or ones are in a 2-digit number. For example, 86 is made up of 8 tens (80) and 6 ones (6).

4 Some sunflowers have grown in the garden.

Put the letters of the sunflowers in order from tallest to shortest.

What is the difference in height between
the tallest and shortest sunflower?  cm

5 Ezra has collected some leaves that have fallen off the trees in his garden.

Draw a line of symmetry on each leaf.

Your child needs to be able to identify line symmetry. Look at different objects and patterns (e.g. a pattern on tiles) with your child and discuss whether they are symmetrical.

6 There are 40 plants in a flower bed.

$\frac{1}{4}$ of the plants are roses.

$\frac{1}{2}$ of the plants are ferns.

The rest of the plants are daisies.

How many plants are roses?

How many plants are ferns?

How many plants are daisies?

7 The pictogram shows the number of birds in the garden one morning.

= 2 birds

Robins	
Blackbirds	
Sparrows	
Blue tits	

How many robins were in the garden?

How many more sparrows than blue tits were in the garden?

How many birds were in the garden in total?

8 A cat often comes into the garden.
Use these words to complete the sentences describing the position of the cat.

| in the middle of | under | on top of | near |

The cat is _____ _____ the fence.

The cat is _____ the table.

The cat is _____ the pond.

The cat is _____ _____ the lawn.

Help your child to use positional language: talk with them using language such as left and right, top, middle and bottom, on top of, in front of, above, between, around, near, close and far, up and down, forwards and backwards, inside and outside.

Playing games

You are having fun playing games with your family and friends. You can work out scores, recognise odd and even numbers and keep track of points.

1 You and your friends are playing 'First to 100'.
Add the number shown on the spinner to each player's score.

Zoe: 87 + 🎯 = ☐

Leo: 92 + 🎯 = ☐

Raj: 88 + 🎯 = ☐

Tom: 96 + 🎯 = ☐

Who is the first player to get to 100? _____

2 You are playing a number card game. Here are your cards.

Choose two cards to make the **highest** possible number.
Write your answer in words.

_____

Choose two cards to make the **lowest** possible number.
Write your answer in words.

_____

30

3 You are playing bingo.
This is your bingo card.

7	22	42	52	69
11	29	34	51	74
4	25	FREE	55	63
12	23	44	50	72
9	19	37	57	64

Circle all the numbers that are **even.**

Colour all the numbers that are in the 5 times table.

What is the **difference** between the largest and smallest number on the card?

4 You are playing a computer game.

You score 37 points in Level 1. You score 65 points in Level 2.

How many points do you score in total?

For every 10 points, you get 1 star.
How many stars do you get?

Your child needs to know how to identify odd and even numbers. Discuss with your child how even numbers can always be divided equally into two and end with the digit 0, 2, 4, 6, 8. Also, look at how odd numbers always end with the digit 1, 3, 5, 7 or 9.

Answers

Page 4–7

1. 20p, 2p, 2p circled; 50p, 20p, 2p circled; 20p, 10p, 1p circled; 50p, 10p, 2p circled
2. Coins drawn must add up to £3 and 75p
3. 400 g; 500 g; 700 g; 1 kg; 2 kg; 1.5 kg
4. circled; circled; circled
5. £2; £1; 50p; £3
6. 50p, 45p, 90p; 50p, 55p, 10p
   Various answers acceptable

Pages 8–11

1. 1 – **First**; 2 – **Secondly**; 3 – **Thirdly**; 4 – **Next**; 5 – **After that** (or: 4 – **After that**; 5 – **Next**); 6 – **Finally**
2.
3. cuboid; cylinder; sphere
4. Tuesday and Friday
5. In any order: A with C; A with D; B with C; B with D
6. Bus number 17 circled; 20 minutes; 15 minutes
7. Start; Forward 4; Right 6; Forward 3; Left 3

Pages 12–15

1. March; April; May; June; July; October; December
   Spring – March, April, May; Summer – June, July, August; Autumn – September, October, November; Winter – December, January, February
2. 14 days; 6 days; 8 days; 2 days; 2 days; 6 days
   14 days were sunny. Half of 30 days is 15 days.
3. Dublin – 15°C; London – 20°C;
   Oslo – 10°C; Dubai – 40°C; Berlin – 25°C;
   Athens – accept 27°C, 28°C or 29°C
   Dubai, Athens, Berlin, London; 20°C
4. Bar drawn to 125 ml for January; June; March and April; 450 ml
5. 75; 25

Pages 16–17

1. 2 cm; 5 cm; 3.5 cm
2. Any 1 part shaded, e.g.
   Any 7 parts shaded, e.g.
3. 11 o'clock; half past one; quarter past 4
   40 kg; 80 kg; 100 kg; 200 kg
4. <; >; >; <

Pages 18–19

1. Bread and pasta – bread, spaghetti
   Fruit and vegetables – broccoli, carrot, orange, banana
   Meat and beans (protein) – chicken, beans
   Dairy – cheese, milk, yoghurt, (butter)
   Fats and oils – oil, (butter)

2. Sophie – 8, 10, 12, 14, 16, 18, 20
   Billy – 40, 50, 60, 70, 80, 90, 100
3. 18; 25; 1; 6; 35

Pages 20–21

1. A: 60p; B: 92p; C: 27p
   A: 40p; B: 8p; C: 73p
2. Jar B; 6; No, they do not have enough money in them.
3. 50 coins; 100 coins; 9 coins; 10 coins
4. £50; 10 weeks
5. £10

Pages 22–25

1. first jug circled; middle jug circled; middle jug circled; 1000 ml; 10 glasses
2. 600 g of oats, 160 g of butter, 120 g of syrup
   150 g of oats, 40 g of butter, 30 g of syrup
   450 g of oats, 120 g of butter, 90 g of syrup
3.
   12:50 pm / 10 minutes to 1 o'clock
4. $4 \times 2 = 8$; $2 \times 4 = 8$; $3 \times 5 = 15$; $5 \times 3 = 15$; $4 \times 5 = 20$; $5 \times 4 = 20$
5. Ten minutes to three o'clock / 2:50 pm;
   Twenty five minutes to 4 / Three thirty-five / 3:35 pm
6. $\frac{4}{8}$ or $\frac{1}{2}$
7.
8. 50 strawberries; 5 boxes; £6

Pages 26–29

1.
2. 7; 10
3. 30; 20
4. C, A, B, D, E; 24 cm
5.
6. 10 roses; 20 ferns; 10 daisies
7. 4; 4; 20
8. on top of; under; near; in the middle of

Pages 30–31

1. Zoe – 92; Leo – 95; Raj – 94; Tom – 100; Tom
2. ninety-three; thirteen
3. 22, 42, 52, 34, 74, 4, 12, 44, 50, 72, 64 circled
   25, 55, 50 coloured; 70 (74 − 4)
4. 102; 10